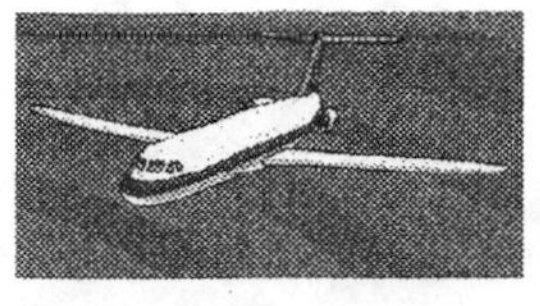

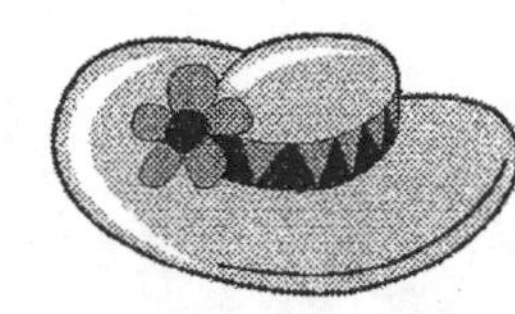

Word Search & Crossword Puzzles Assessment Sheets & Solutions

For The Children's Picture-Word & Simple Sentence Book

By

Dr. Harry R. Irving, Ed. D.

Cover Illustrations By Graphics Factory

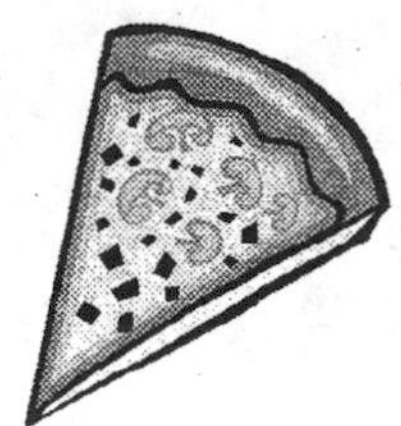

Fully Reproducible

Primary Grades & ESOL Students

Table of Contents

Crossword Puzzles (18)

Word Search Solutions (18)

Crossword Solutions (18)

Introduction

.

The book is designed to assist parents and teachers in developing Children's Language Arts Skills, at home and at the school's primary grade levels.

Primarily, this Assessment Book, consisting of eighteen word search and eighteen crossword puzzles sheets and solutions was developed by the author to accompany the author's " A Children's Picture-Word and Simple Sentence Book " and to evaluate what the child has learned.

Also this book is designed for English for Speakers of Other Languages (ESOL) students.

Further the author grants teachers permission to photocopy the pages from this book for classroom use.

Finally, below is a list of the author's works that are a must and parents, teachers, and students are encouraged to purchase them. Each sold separately.

1) **"Children's Picture-Word and Simple Sentence Book"**
2) **"Picture Coloring Book"**
3) **"Word Search and Crossword Puzzles Book"**
4) **"Picture-Word Quizzes Book"**
5) **"Flip Charts and Name Tags Packet"**

Name ____________________________

Subject __________________________

Date ____________________________

Teacher __________________________

A Children's Picture-Word and Simple Sentence Book Word Search Puzzle

Find the words in the grid. Words can go horizontally, vertically and diagonally in all eight directions.

S N O O L L A B R E B
R A L W L Q N O Y N T
Z S P R P K T T R A K
N W A E G A L K M L N
R E T N G A N T B P M
B Q F I A M X N J R V
H L L A B N B H H I W
B L F P L A A M K A T
A B G P L N C B K G A
T L K L C Y L V N W B
L T G E B G L J L G L

airplane
alligator
ant
ape
apple
ball
balloons
bananas
bat
bear

Name ________________________ Date _________

A Children's Picture-Word and Simple Sentence Book Crossword Puzzle

1 2 3 4 5 6 7 8 9

Dr. Harry R. Irving, Ed. D. www.CrosswordWeaver.com

ACROSS

3 You can throw me.
5 I am a fruit.
6 I live in the forest.
8 I am an insect.
9 I can fly high in the sky.

DOWN

1 I live in caves.
2 I am a big reptile.
4 They call me a gorilla.
6 You can blow me up.
7 I taste good on cereal.

WORD BANK: Airplane, alligator, ant, ape, apple, ball, balloons, bananas, bat, bear.

Name ______________________________

Subject ____________________________

Date ______________________________

Teacher ____________________________

A Children's Picture-Word and Simple
Sentence Book Word Search Puzzle

Find the words in the grid. Words can go horizontally, vertically and diagonally in all eight directions.

D	P	L	H	W	M	E	B
A	B	Y	N	P	L	D	U
E	O	N	B	C	R	E	F
R	O	R	Y	O	Q	B	F
B	K	C	Y	T	A	B	A
B	I	R	D	O	O	T	L
B	Q	M	F	X	B	J	O
L	W	O	B	J	M	F	M

bed
bicycle
bird
boat
book
bowl
box
boy
bread
buffalo

Name ______________________ Date _________

A Children's Picture-Word and Simple Sentence Book Crossword Puzzle

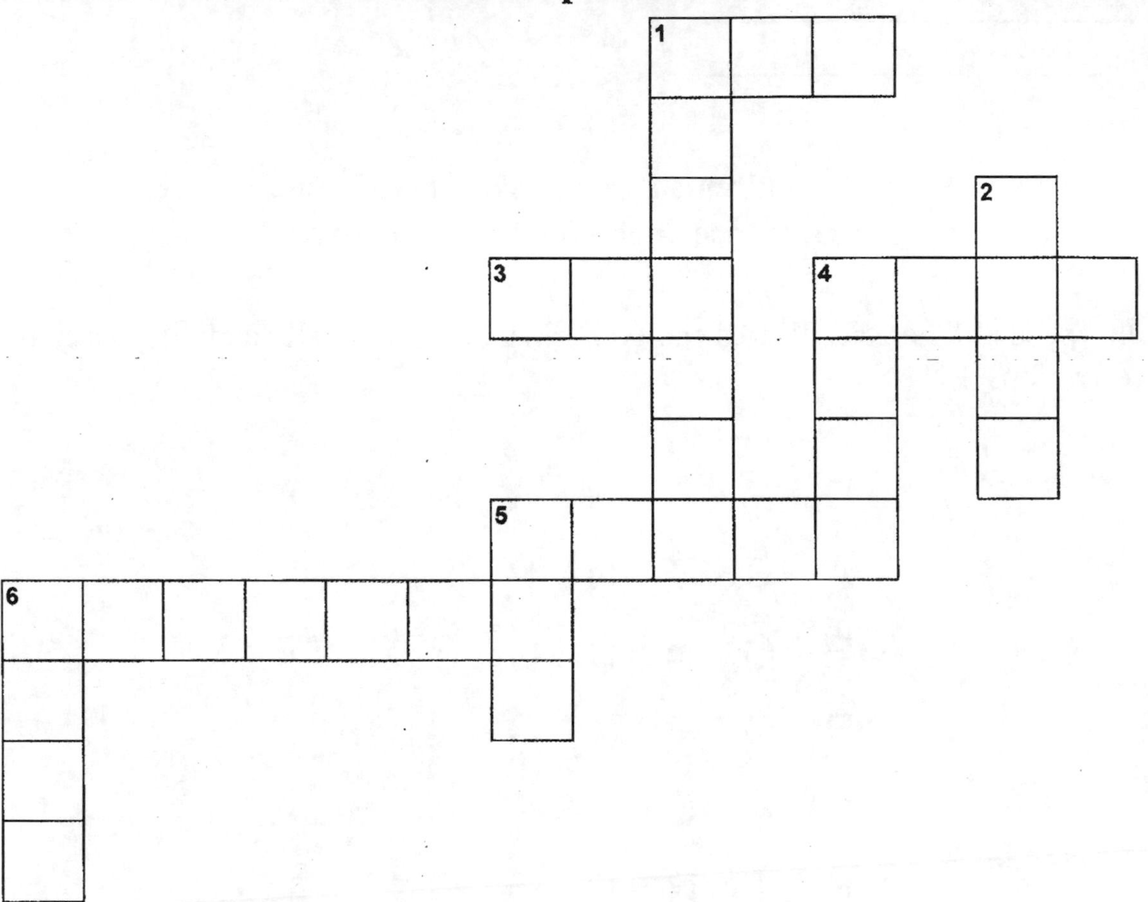

Dr. Harry R. Irving, Ed. D. www.CrosswordWeaver.com

ACROSS

1 You can sleep in me.
3 My name is Juan.
4 You can read me.
5 You can put butter on me.
6 I have horns.

DOWN

1 I have two wheels.
2 You can eat soup in me.
4 I have wings.
5 You can put a gift in me.
6 You can go fishing in me.

WORD BANK: Bed, bicycle, bird, boat, book, bowl, box, boy, bread, buffalo.

Name ____________________________

Subject ___________________________

Date ______________________________

Teacher ___________________________

A Children's Picture-Word and Simple Sentence Book Word Search Puzzle

Find the words in the grid. Words can go horizontally, vertically and diagonally in all eight directions.

T	L	B	T	O	R	R	A	C
E	E	U	B	U	T	T	E	R
L	M	T	M	W	S	K	M	T
D	A	T	N	U	G	R	F	Q
N	C	E	B	L	G	L	W	K
A	M	R	C	V	U	T	T	C
C	K	F	J	A	B	R	A	C
Y	V	L	N	Y	K	P	T	H
K	L	Y	F	T	B	E	X	T

bug
bus
butter
butterfly
cake
camel
candle
cap
car
carrot

Name ______________________ Date ________ 3A

A Children's Picture-Word and Simple Sentence Book Crossword Puzzle

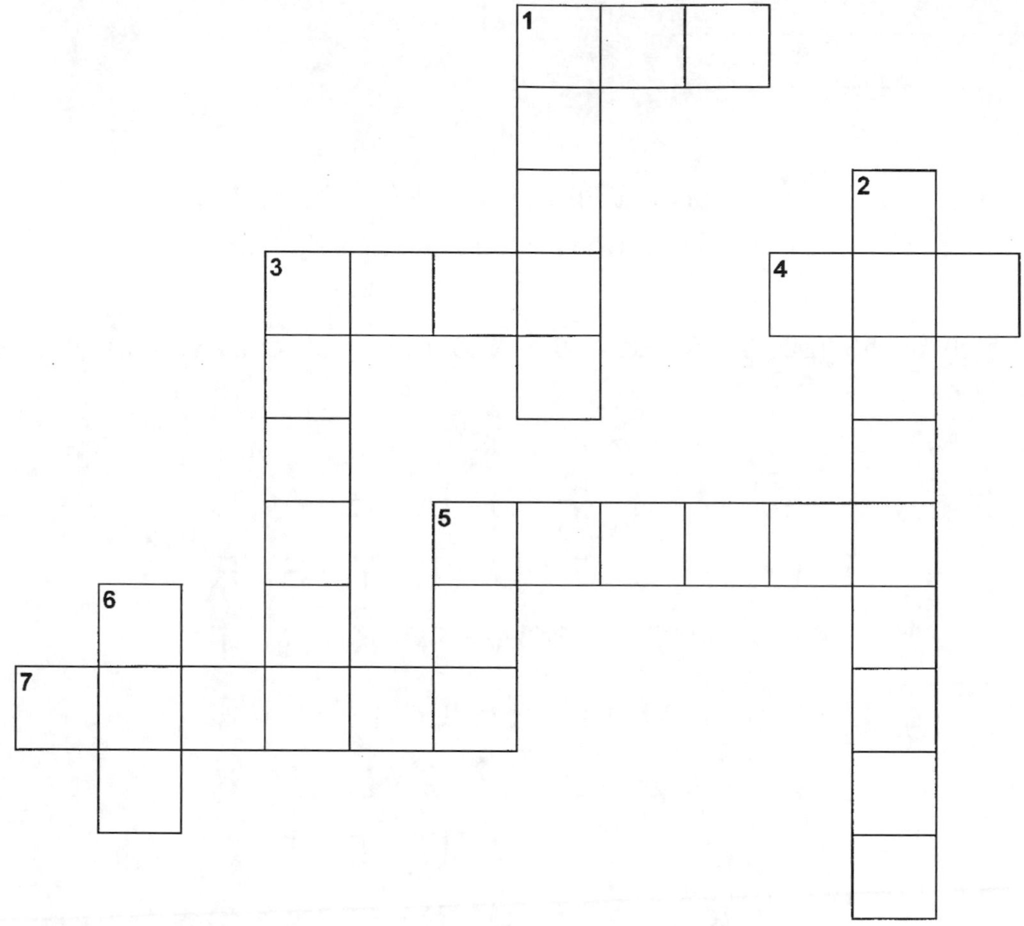

Dr. Harry R. Irving, Ed. D. www.CrosswordWeaver.com

ACROSS

1 You can wear me on your head.
3 I will make your birthday happy.
4 I will take you to school.
5 You can see in the dark with me.
7 You can put me on bread.

DOWN

1 I have one or two humps.
2 I use to be a caterpillar.
3 I am a vegetable.
5 You can ride in me.
6 I can crawl.

WORD BANK: Bug, bus, butter, butterfly, cake, camel, candle, cap, car, carrot.

Name ______________________

Subject ______________________

Date ______________________

Teacher ______________________

A Children's Picture-Word and Simple Sentence Book Word Search Puzzle

Find the words in the grid. Words can go horizontally, vertically and diagonally in all eight directions.

```
R R R K V M L C F K R C
H F T R R H H V H I K H
Y B K Z X I T Z A Y X E
R K F C C Q P H M H X E
E C C K H M C Q R P K S
T L E O K E T J Q P V E
U N H T L L R T N K M B
P L B A M C M R H G T U
M H F C H B M Q Y G V R
O N P N C H E E S E Q G
C Y K C I G A R E T T E
W F M J H C R U H C T R
```


cat
chair
cheese
cheeseburger
cherry
chicken
church
cigarette
clock
computer

Name ____________________ Date ________

A Children's Picture-Word and Simple Sentence Book Crossword Puzzle

Dr. Harry R. Irving, Ed. D. www.CrosswordWeaver.com

ACROSS

1 I say Meow, Meow, Meow.
4 I am a sandwich.
5 I am a fruit.
6 I like visitors on Sundays.
7 Please do not smoke me.
8 I say Cluck, Cluck, Cluck.

DOWN

1 You can do school work on me.
2 You can sit in me.
3 You can tell time with me.
5 I am made from milk.

WORD BANK: Cat, chair, cheese, cheeseburger, cherry, chicken, church, cigarette, clock, computer.

Name ______________________

Subject ______________________

Date ______________________

Teacher ______________________

A Children's Picture-Word and Simple Sentence Book Word Search Puzzle

Find the words in the grid. Words can go horizontally, vertically and diagonally in all eight directions.

N	S	T	C	W	F	H
I	E	Q	D	U	C	D
H	I	L	O	U	P	O
P	K	C	O	W	D	L
L	O	C	R	O	E	L
O	O	L	G	Y	E	L
D	C	S	S	E	R	D

cookies
couch
cow
cup
deer
dog
doll
dolphin
door
dress

Name ________________________ Date _________ 5A

A Children's Picture-Word and Simple Sentence Book Crossword Puzzle

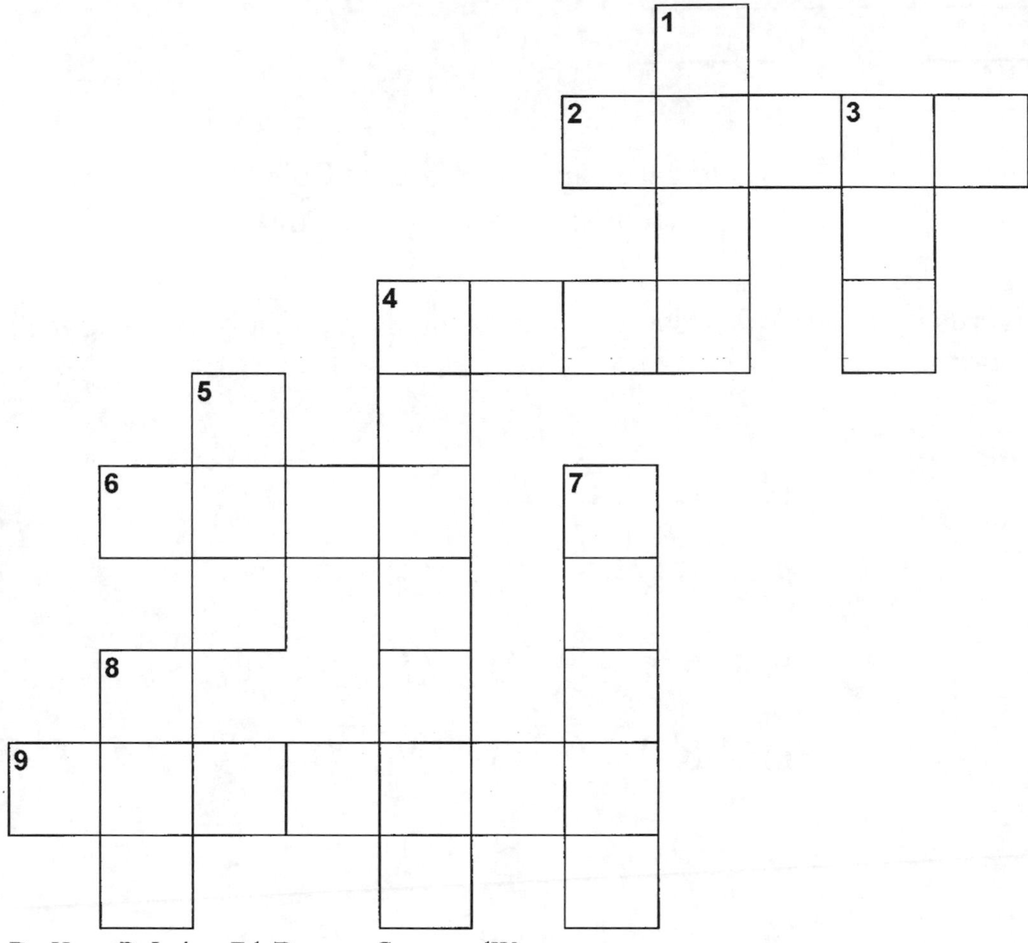

Dr. Harry R. Irving, Ed. D. www.CrosswordWeaver.com

ACROSS

2 You can take a nap on me.
4 I live in the forest.
6 You can play with me.
9 You bake me in the oven.

DOWN

1 You can open me.
3 You can drink coffee out of me.
4 I live in the ocean.
5 I make a good pet.
7 Girls wear me.
8 I say Moo, Moo, Moo.

WORD BANK: Cookies, couch, cow, cup, deer, dog, doll, dolphin, door, dress.

Name ______________________________

Subject ____________________________

Date _______________________________

Teacher ____________________________

A Children's Picture-Word and Simple Sentence Book Word Search Puzzle

Find the words in the grid. Words can go horizontally, vertically and diagonally in all eight directions.

```
E T N A H P E L E
R Y H S C P N B R
G E E M E A G L E
G D A U J N K V V
E R E R L C D E R
G L C D U L I E N
G R N D M G R F Z
S Q E C H I G X B
N Q F T F P R K T
```


drums
duck
eagle
ear
eggs
eight
elephant
eye
fence
fire

Name ______________________ Date ________ 6A

A Children's Picture-Word and Simple Sentence Book Crossword Puzzle

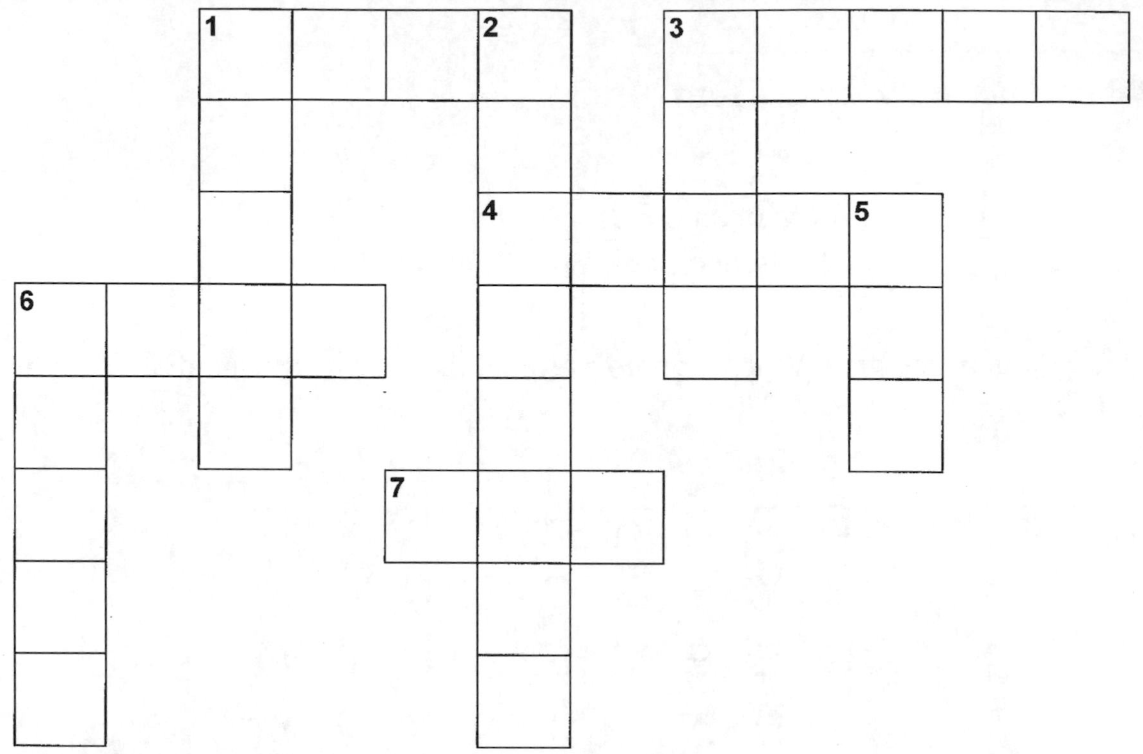

Dr. Harry R. Irving, Ed. D. www.CrosswordWeaver.com

ACROSS

1 I am extremely hot.
3 I am a number.
4 I can fly high in the sky.
6 I say Quack, Quack, Quack.
7 You hear with me.

DOWN

1 You can put me around your yard.
2 I have a long trunk.
3 You can boil me.
5 You can see with me.
6 I am a musical instrument.

WORD BANK: Drums, duck, eagle, ear, eggs, eight, elephant, eye, fence, fire.

Name ______________________________

Subject ______________________________

Date ______________________________

Teacher ______________________________

A Children's Picture-Word and Simple
Sentence Book Word Search Puzzle

Find the words in the grid. Words can go horizontally, vertically and diagonally in all eight directions.

N	M	K	M	N	K	P	W	M	S	B
B	K	F	Z	N	Z	G	B	H	E	Z
Y	L	N	Z	D	V	G	K	M	I	L
F	L	A	G	V	O	H	N	K	R	G
H	Y	J	K	R	K	S	T	R	F	D
B	F	M	F	Z	Y	I	G	R	H	Z
D	G	L	E	M	F	F	H	Y	C	R
N	F	V	O	O	X	W	R	Y	N	F
M	I	G	R	W	X	O	Z	N	E	L
F	N	K	Q	D	E	V	F	Q	R	Y
K	C	R	U	O	F	R	Y	H	F	K

fish
five
flag
flower
fly
fork
four
fox
french fries
frog

Name ______________________ Date _________ 7A

A Children's Picture-Word and Simple Sentence Book Crossword Puzzle

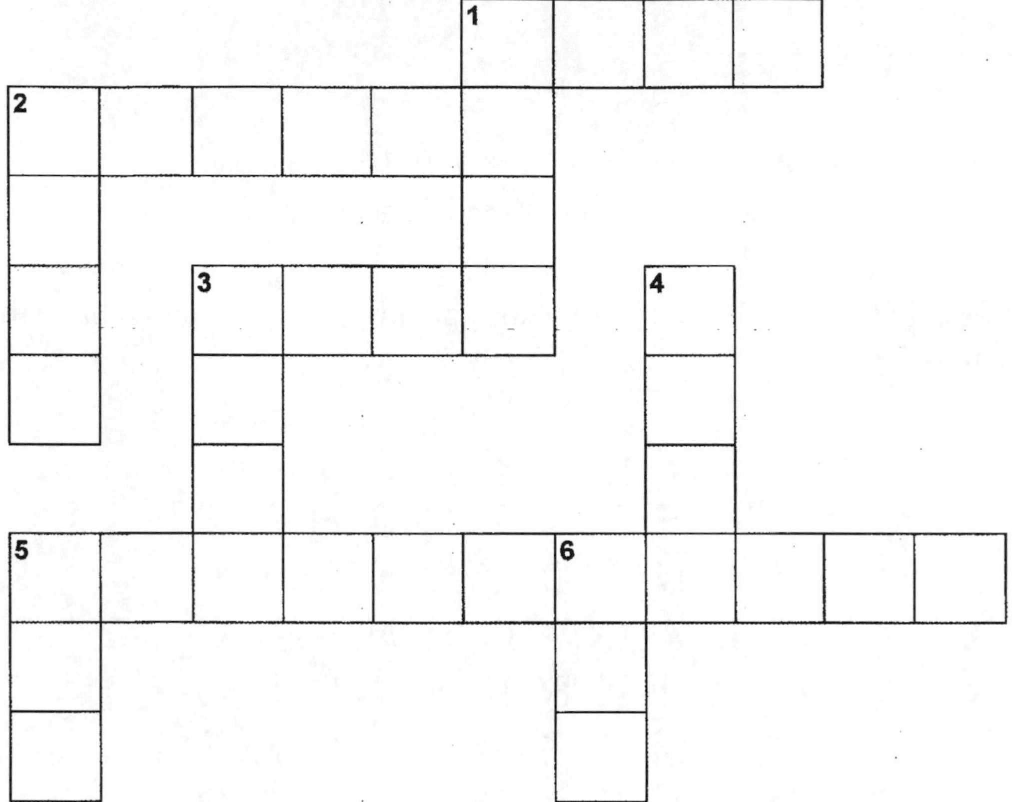

Dr. Harry R. Irving, Ed. D. www.CrosswordWeaver.com

ACROSS

1 You can eat me.
2 I am a plant.
3 I am red, white, and blue.
5 I am made from potatoes.

DOWN

1 I am an amphibian.
2 You can eat with me.
3 I am a number.
4 I am a number
5 I live in the forest.
6 I am an insect.

WORD BANK: Fish, five, flag, flower, fly, fork, four, fox, frenchfries, frog.

Name ____________________

Subject ____________________

Date ____________________

Teacher ____________________

A Children's Picture-Word and Simple Sentence Book Word Search Puzzle

Find the words in the grid. Words can go horizontally, vertically and diagonally in all eight directions.

K	R	M	B	N	Y	E	W	Z	P
S	E	P	A	R	G	T	Z	P	N
X	G	M	K	L	L	A	G	E	G
C	R	N	Q	H	M	G	F	T	L
F	U	J	N	N	M	F	A	C	O
H	B	G	G	U	A	H	X	M	V
Q	M	O	L	R	G	M	K	Y	E
J	A	M	I	A	G	I	R	L	S
T	H	G	V	N	S	Q	T	J	K
C	C	Z	D	B	Y	S	Z	W	D

gate
giraffe
girl
glass
gloves
goat
grapes
gun
hamburger
hat

Name ______________________ Date _________

A Children's Picture-Word and Simple Sentence Book Crossword Puzzle

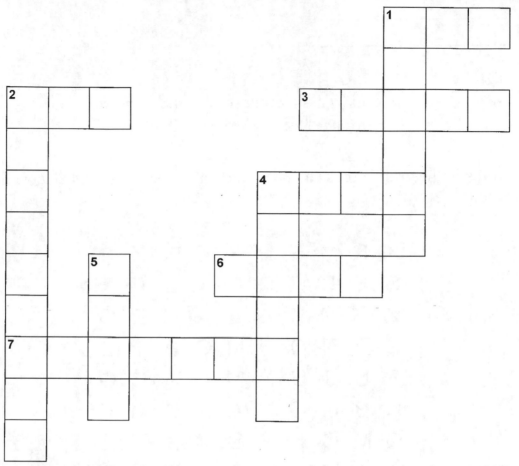

Dr. Harry R. Irving, Ed. D. www.CrosswordWeaver.com

ACROSS

1 I am dangerous.
2 You can wear me on your head.
3 You can drink water out of me.
4 I will not let the dog out.
6 I have horns.
7 I have a long neck

DOWN

1 I grow on a vine.
2 I am made from meat.
4 I will keep your hands warm.
5 My name is Nancy.

WORD BANK: Gate, giraffe, girl, glass, gloves, goat, grapes, gun, hamburger, hat.

Name ______________________________

Subject ____________________________

Date _______________________________

Teacher ____________________________

A Children's Picture-Word and Simple Sentence Book Word Search Puzzle

Find the words in the grid. Words can go horizontally, vertically and diagonally in all eight directions.

```
L J L W Z E C I U J H
T O N I W W F C E K G
T L O N C Q H T W J E
M K J R D E I K E D S
T Q A Z A K C L P G R
F Y C D J G L R O L O
Y E K M J Y N D E J H
Z K E B F F T A T A R
R B T I N O K G K N M
R N S Q H R M L N M K
Z H Z H O U S E V V T
```


horse
hot dog
house
ice cream
jacket
jellyfish
juice
kangaroo
key
kite

Name ______________________ Date ________

A Children's Picture-Word and Simple Sentence Book Crossword Puzzle

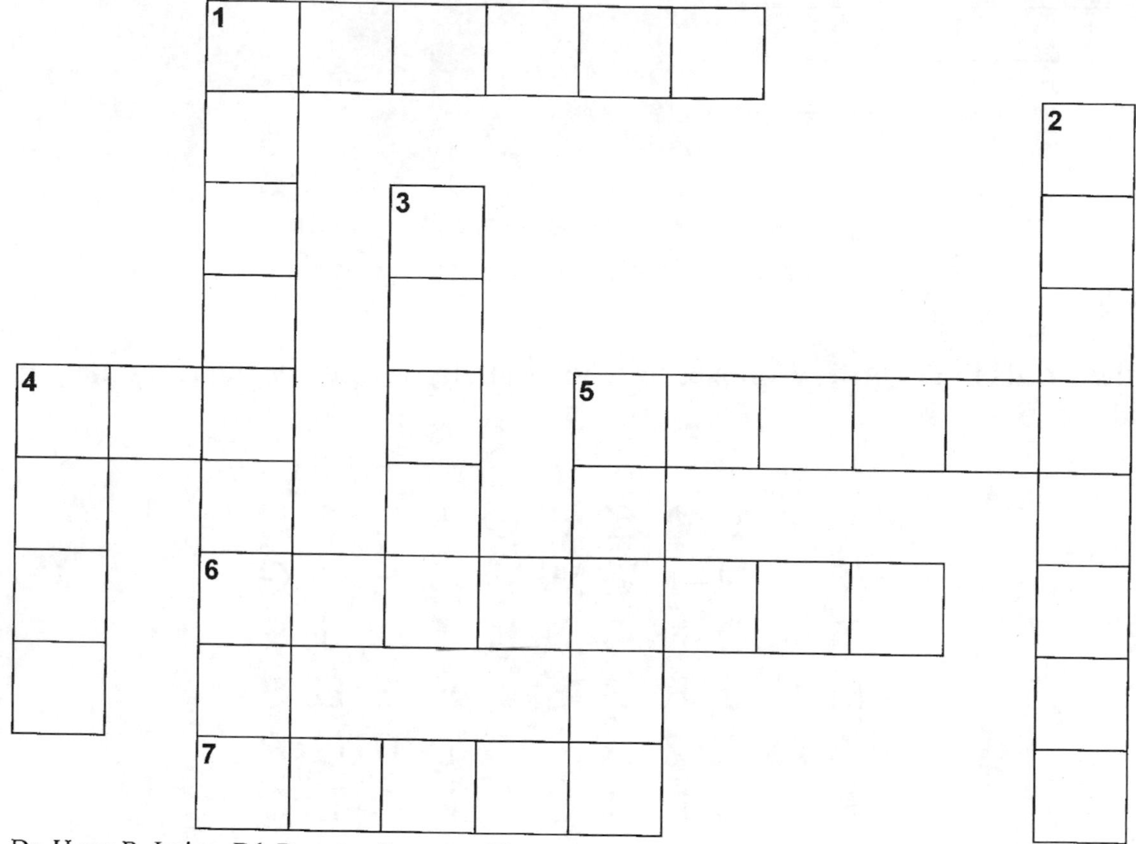

Dr. Harry R. Irving, Ed. D. www.CrosswordWeaver.com

ACROSS

1 I can keep you warm.
4 You need me to open doors.
5 You can put mustard on me.
6 You can eat me on a cone.
7 You can live in me.

DOWN

1 I live in the ocean.
2 I live in Australia.
3 I am made from oranges.
4 I can fly high in the sky.
5 I can run really fast.

WORD BANK: Horse, hotdog, house, icecream, jacket, jellyfish, juice, kangaroo, key, kite.

Name ______________________________

Subject ____________________________

Date ______________________________

Teacher ____________________________

A Children's Picture-Word and Simple Sentence Book Word Search Puzzle

Find the words in the grid. Words can go horizontally, vertically and diagonally in all eight directions.

D	T	F	E	C	U	T	T	E	L
L	K	L	L	A	D	D	E	R	N
D	G	J	A	N	P	F	N	E	E
R	V	K	N	M	O	K	F	L	T
A	P	D	C	V	P	I	E	L	T
Z	R	P	K	W	N	O	L	E	I
I	N	T	F	K	P	V	T	M	K
L	C	N	T	A	B	B	R	O	M
P	A	K	R	R	D	M	L	N	D
M	K	D	L	K	K	M	N	C	K

kitten
knife
ladder
lamp
lemon
leopard
lettuce
lion
lizard
man

Name ______________________ Date ________

A Children's Picture-Word and Simple Sentence Book Crossword Puzzle

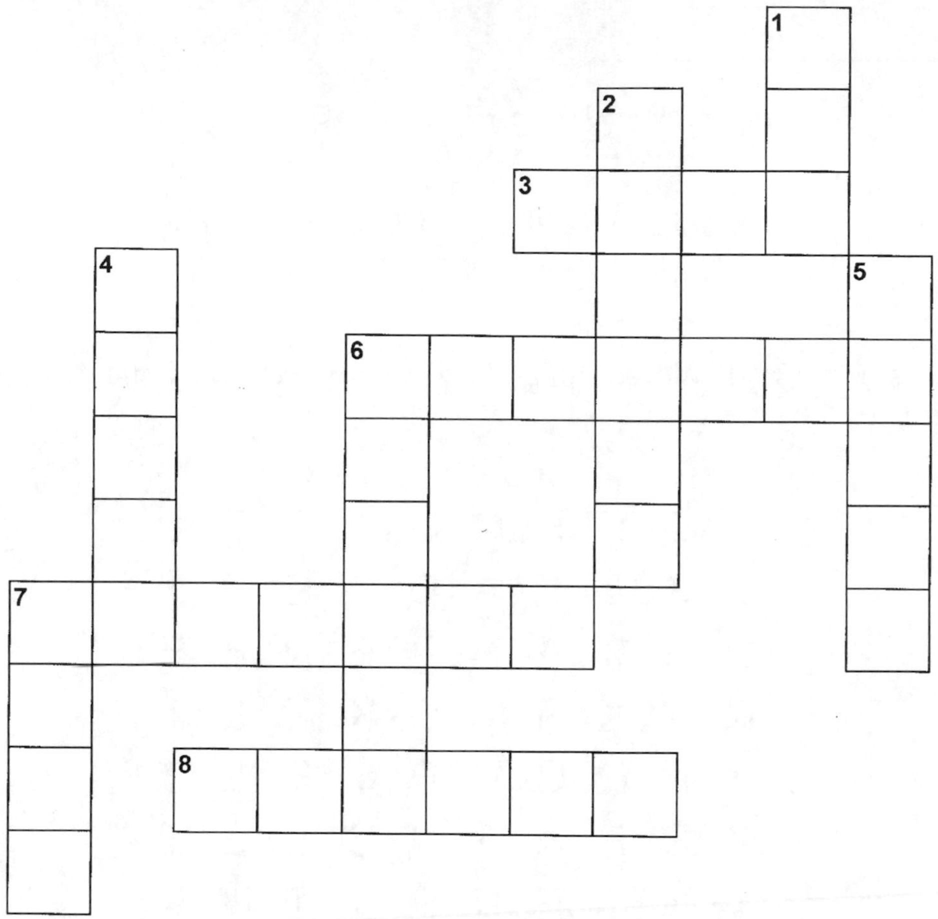

ACROSS

3 I am king of the jungle.
6 I am a green vegetable.
7 I can run really fast.
8 You can reach high places on me.

DOWN

1 My name is Jose.
2 I am a little baby cat.
4 You can cut a cake with me.
5 You can make lemonade out of me.
6 I am a reptile.
7 Please turn me off when you go to bed.

WORD BANK: Kitten, knife, ladder, lamp, lemon, leopard, lettuce, lion, lizard, man.

Name ____________________________

Subject __________________________

Date ____________________________

Teacher __________________________

A Children's Picture-Word and Simple Sentence Book Word Search Puzzle

Find the words in the grid. Words can go horizontally, vertically and diagonally in all eight directions.

```
R M G S K E S U O M G
R L O X U H L B Y M X
K Z J N X P B V O T D
K B D Z K E O T G M F
P T T Y G E O T M Y M
A D Y N P R Y K C D M
M Q A B C R L N M O F
P R K Y R I M C O Y T
O Q C R M H J J O E D
K L B M O N E Y S N L
E V N T T J P T E O T
```


map
milk
money
monkey
moose
motorcycle
mouse
octopus
one
orange

Name ______________________ Date ________

A Children's Picture-Word and Simple Sentence Book Crossword Puzzle

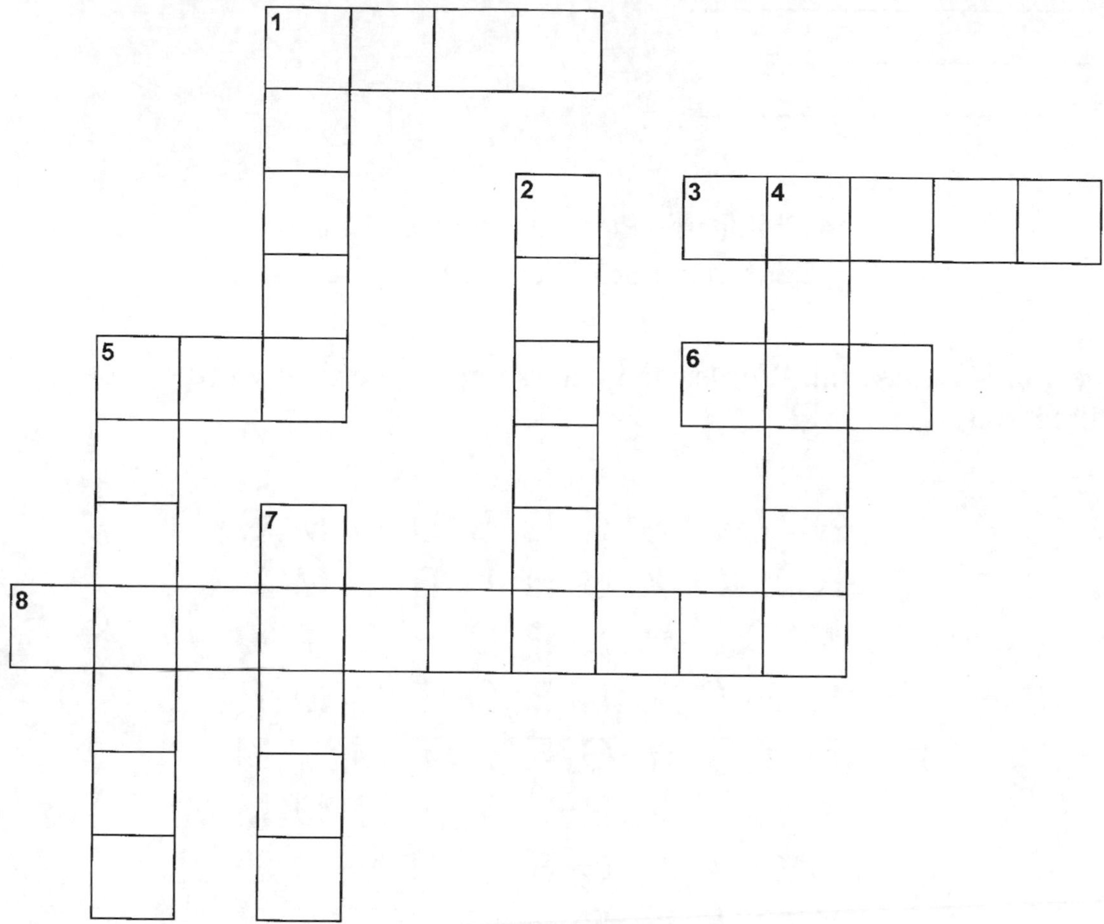

Dr. Harry R. Irving, Ed. D. www.CrosswordWeaver.com

ACROSS

1 I come from cows.
3 You can save me in the bank.
5 I am a number.
6 I am a drawing of the United States.
8 I have two wheels.

DOWN

1 I like cheese
2 I like bananas.
4 I am a fruit.
5 I have eight arms.
7 I have antlers.

WORD BANK: Map, milk, money, monkey, moose, motorcycle, mouse, octopus, one, orange.

Name ______________________________

Subject ____________________________

Date ______________________________

Teacher ____________________________

A Children's Picture-Word and Simple Sentence Book Word Search Puzzle

Find the words in the grid. Words can go horizontally, vertically and diagonally in all eight directions.

P	L	W	E	R	M	J	M	L
E	S	L	I	C	N	E	P	L
A	G	Z	P	P	A	N	T	S
C	H	L	V	A	P	K	H	N
H	O	T	R	E	R	W	T	H
F	L	N	A	F	L	R	G	D
V	W	R	A	N	W	W	O	G
Y	X	L	A	I	O	T	I	T
D	L	P	H	B	P	P	X	H

owl
pan
pants
parrot
peach
pear
pencils
piano
pie
pig

Name ____________________ Date ________

A Children's Picture-Word and Simple Sentence Book Crossword Puzzle

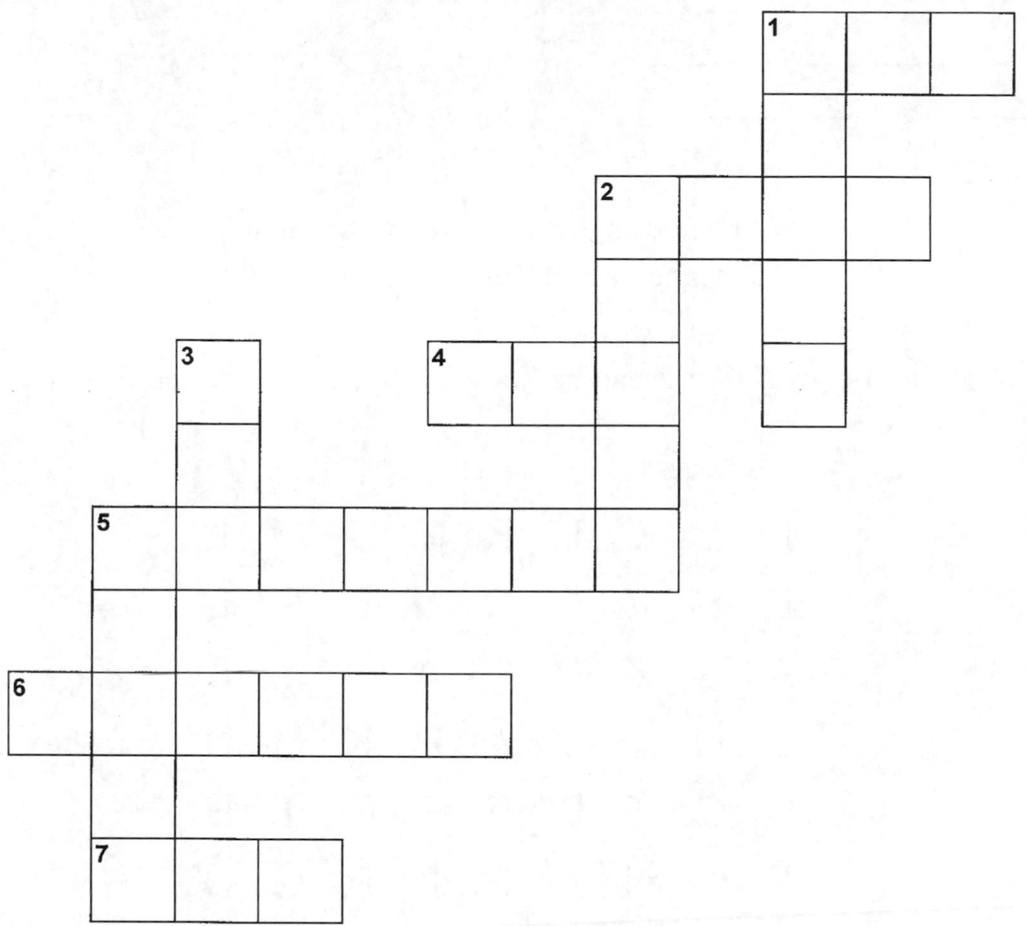

Dr. Harry R. Irving, Ed. D. www.CrosswordWeaver.com

ACROSS

1 I say Oink, Oink, Oink.
2 I rhyme with bear.
4 You can fry eggs in me.
5 You can write with me.
6 I can talk.
7 I say Woo, Woo, Woo.

DOWN

1 You can make a pie out of me.
2 You can wear me.
3 I am a desert.
5 I am a musical instrument.

WORD BANK: Owl, pan, pants, parrot, peach, pear, pencils, piano, pie, pig.

Name ______________________________

Subject ____________________________

Date ______________________________

Teacher ____________________________

A Children's Picture-Word and Simple Sentence Book Word Search Puzzle

Find the words in the grid. Words can go horizontally, vertically and diagonally in all eight directions.

```
C E P N G C L C V L T
T L H O L P L A T E S
I P T L O W Y B M H V
B P R P P L Q P N B Q
B A D R O T T O P M F
A E H Y T P O A A U R
R N B T O C W Z B Y P
T I W T C G Z L Q L W
K P A A H I K C L M E
R T R D P B Z J K Q K
O Z N I K P M U P R H
```


pineapple
pizza
plates
pool table
pot
potato
pumpkin
puppy
rabbit
raccoon

Name ________________________ Date _________

A Children's Picture-Word and Simple Sentence Book Crossword Puzzle

1 2 3 4 5 6 7 8

Dr. Harry R. Irving, Ed. D. www.CrosswordWeaver.com

ACROSS

1 I am a little baby dog.
3 I will visit you on Halloween.
4 You can make French fries out of me.
6 You eat food out of me.
8 I can jump.

DOWN

1 I grow in Hawaii.
2 You can cook in me.
3 You can play pool on me.
5 I hunt for food at night.
7 I came to America from Italy.

WORD BANK: Pineapple, pizza, plates, pooltable, pot, potato, pumpkin, puppy, rabbit, raccoon.

Name ____________________

Subject ____________________

Date ____________________

Teacher ____________________

A Children's Picture-Word and Simple Sentence Book Word Search Puzzle

Find the words in the grid. Words can go horizontally, vertically and diagonally in all eight directions.

S	T	P	L	Z	J	C	Z	P
M	C	H	I	K	R	A	H	S
Y	V	H	N	H	V	H	E	T
G	T	P	O	D	S	V	A	T
R	C	E	I	O	E	R	R	H
N	C	E	D	N	L	I	Z	S
T	T	H	A	J	H	M	W	E
G	P	S	R	S	K	M	T	A
Q	W	R	I	N	G	M	M	L

radio
rat
ring
school
seal
seven
shark
sheep
ship
shirt

Name ______________________ Date ________

A Children's Picture-Word and Simple Sentence Book Crossword Puzzle

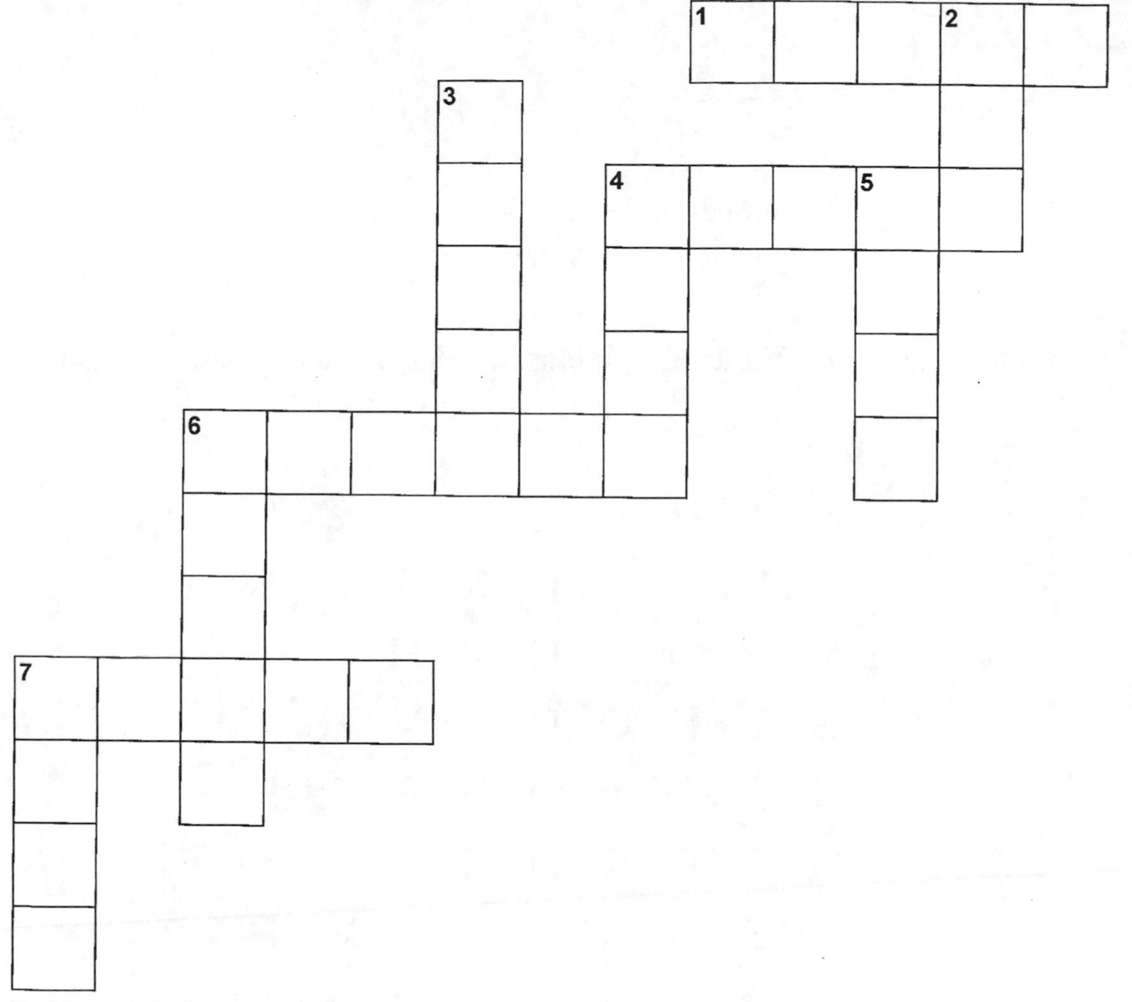

Dr. Harry R. Irving, Ed. D. www.CrosswordWeaver.com

ACROSS

1 I am a big fish.
4 You can wear me.
6 You can learn how to read here.
7 I say Baa, Baa, Baa.

DOWN

2 I like cheese.
3 You can listen to music on me.
4 I have fur.
5 You can wear me on your finger.
6 5+2 = me.
7 You can take a cruise on me.

WORD BANK: Radio, rat, ring, school, seal, seven, shark, sheep, ship, shirt.

Name ______________________

Subject ______________________

Date ______________________

Teacher ______________________

A Children's Picture-Word and Simple
Sentence Book Word Search Puzzle

Find the words in the grid. Words can go horizontally, vertically and diagonally in all eight directions.

```
H Q L D H F Y K B R S
T M X V L R J N J X R
S K E L E T O N Y T A
B Q L N N X W S K S T
B V K O I S H E M K S
K S O S N L M O H U D
M P K A Y S J H H N N
S K I I M J K S P K A
M L Y T R T X C C N Y
B R K B X T K T O P K
C X H E K A N S T S S
```


shoes
six
skeleton
skirt
skunk
sky and stars
snail
snake
socks
spoon

Name ______________________ Date ________

A Children's Picture-Word and Simple Sentence Book Crossword Puzzle

1 2

3

4

5

6

7

8

Dr. Harry R. Irving, Ed. D. www.CrosswordWeaver.com

ACROSS

1 You wear me on your feet.
4 I give off a bad odor.
5 You can eat soup with me
6 Girls wear me.
7 3+3 = me.
8 At night you can see stars in me.

DOWN

2 Milk will make me strong.
3 I am a reptile.
4 I move very slowly.
5 You wear socks with me.

WORD BANK: Shoes, six, skeleton, skirt, skunk, sky, snail, snake, socks, spoon.

Name ______________________

Subject ______________________

Date ______________________

Teacher ______________________

A Children's Picture-Word and Simple Sentence Book Word Search Puzzle

Find the words in the grid. Words can go horizontally, vertically and diagonally in all eight directions.

```
Y S E S S A L G N U S V
Z D N T T N C T M X E D
S U N E W Z E P E L N L
Z H M D V N F V Q E O J
X T B D L W O Y Y R H M
C H A Y N T R R C R P L
M N Z B S T K X W I E L
M L C E L Y B D R U L L
X C L A N E D B Z Q E J
P R X R C M Z X G S T W
L O O P G N I M M I W S
R D N O I S I V E L E T
```


squirrel
stove
sun
sunglasses
swimming pool
table
teddy bear
telephone
television
ten

Name ________________________ Date _________ 16A

A Children's Picture-Word and Simple Sentence Book Crossword Puzzle

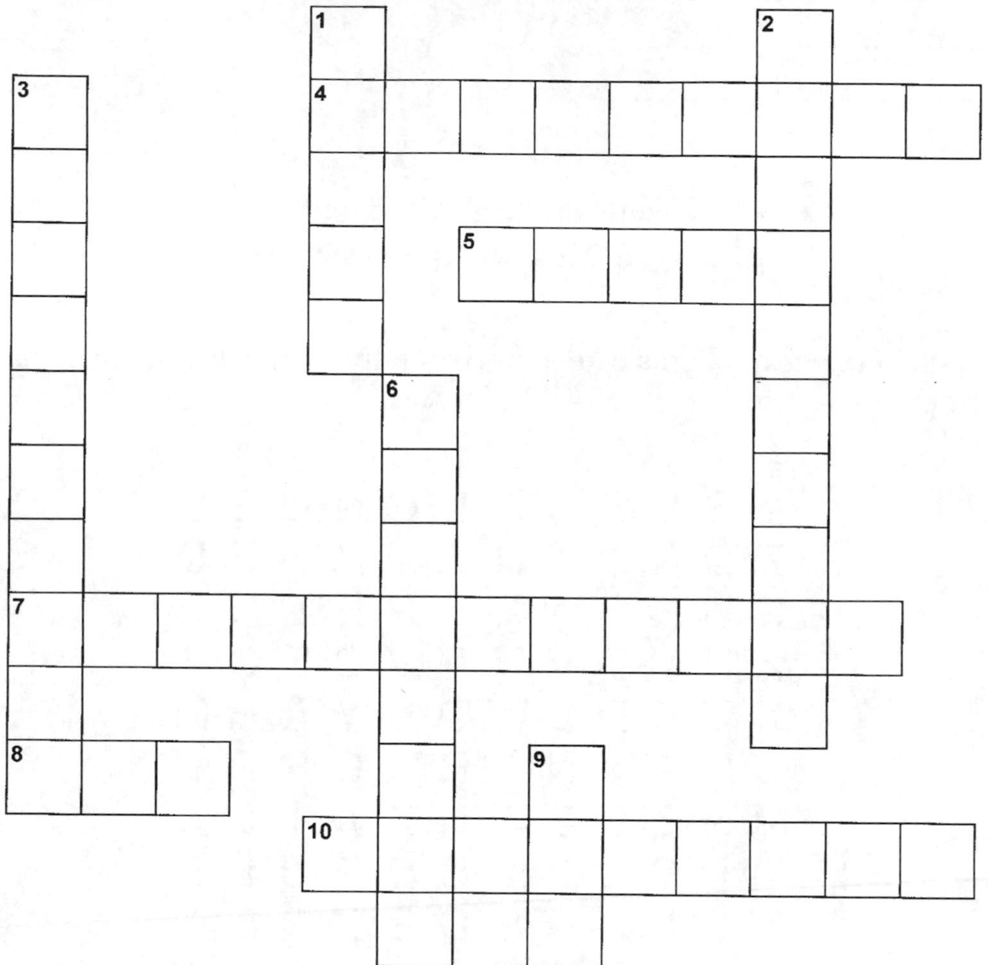

Dr. Harry R. Irving, Ed. D. www.CrosswordWeaver.com

ACROSS

4 Please give me a hug.
5 You can eat dinner on me.
7 They put chlorine in me.
8 I come out in the sky during the day time.
10 You can call your friend with me.

DOWN

1 You can roast a turkey in me.
2 You can watch cartoons on me.
3 Please wear me on a sunny day.
6 I like to eat nuts.
9 9+1= me.

WORD BANK: Squirrel, stove, sun, sunglasses, swimmingpool, table, teddybear, telephone, television, ten.

Name ______________________

Subject ______________________

Date ______________________

Teacher ______________________

A Children's Picture-Word and Simple Sentence Book Word Search Puzzle

Find the words in the grid. Words can go horizontally, vertically and diagonally in all eight directions.

```
M T L W M T E H R X R
T M E L D L N E T L R
Z O R P T N G X E T V
Y B O R M I Y G E T Z
E Q U T T U W F R T R
K T V J H N R E H R B
R Z X N G B E T T A M
U M L D G Q R N K I L
T O M A T O P U H N L
J D T T T T K P S B F
Q C D Q K C U R T H L
```


three
tiger
tomato
toothbrush
train
tree
truck
trumpet
turkey
turtle

Name ________________________ Date ________

A Children's Picture-Word and Simple Sentence Book Crossword Puzzle

1 2 3 4 5 6 7 8

Dr. Harry R. Irving, Ed. D. www.CrosswordWeaver.com

ACROSS

2 See you on Thanksgiving Day.
4 You can clean your teeth with me.
5 I have lots of leaves.
6 You can put me in a salad.
7 1+1+1= me.
8 You can carry stuff in me.

DOWN

1 I live in a shell.
3 I am a musical instrument.
5 I run on railroad tracks.
6 I have stripes.

WORD BANK: Three, tiger, tomato, toothbrush, train, tree, truck, trumpet, turkey, turtle.

Name ____________________

Subject ____________________

Date ____________________

Teacher ____________________

A Children's Picture-Word and Simple
Sentence Book Word Search Puzzle

Find the words in the grid. Words can go horizontally, vertically and diagonally in all eight directions.

```
N G V A S E W A P A
W O J O V Y L V R Y
O F L Q L L N B T D
D T J E E C E R W Q
N D P R M Z A W A G
I D B H J R H N G W
W M R G M A E R O R
U H O N L M N T N R
D X W E K T D Y A G
R L T R N A M O W W
```


two
umbrella
vase
volcano
wagon
watermelon
whale
window
woman
zebra

Name ____________________ Date ________

A Children's Picture-Word and Simple Sentence Book Crossword Puzzle

1 2 3 4 5 6 7 8 9

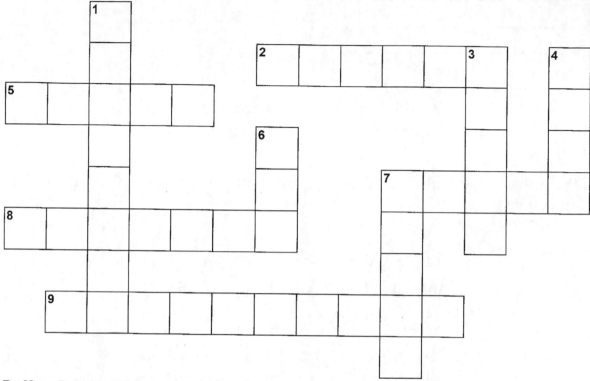

Dr. Harry R. Irving, Ed. D. www.CrosswordWeaver.com

ACROSS

2 You can cover me with blinds.
5 I have stripes.
7 I am a big mammal.
8 I give off lava.
9 I am a fruit.

DOWN

1 I will keep the rain off of you.
3 I am a mother.
4 You can put flowers in me.
6 3-1= me.
7 Kids like to ride in me.

WORD BANK: Two, umbrella, vase, volcano, wagon, watermelon, whale, window, woman, zebra.

A Children's Picture-Word and Simple Sentence Book Word Search Puzzle

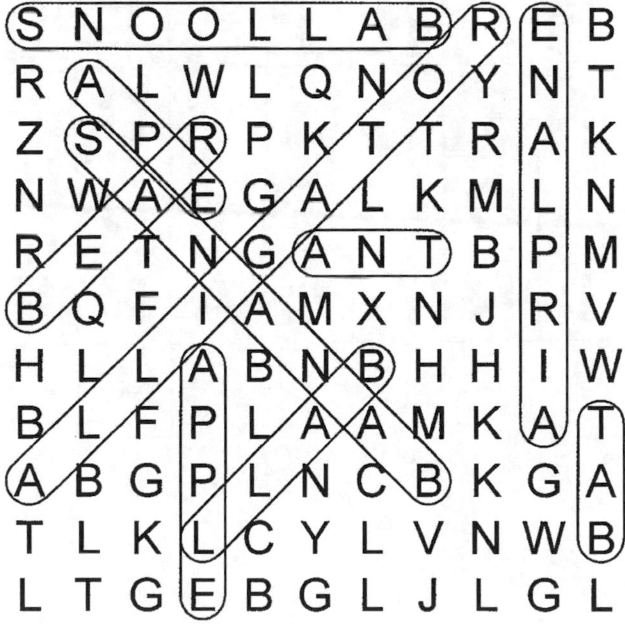

A Children's Picture-Word and Simple Sentence Book Crossword Puzzle

Solution:

B			A				B	A	L	L
A	P	P	L	E				P		
T			L				B	E	A	R
	B		I				A			
	A		G				L			
	N		A	N	T		L			
	A		T				O			
	N		O				O			
	A	I	R	P	L	A	N	E		
	S						S			

A Children's Picture-Word and Simple Sentence Book Word Search Puzzle

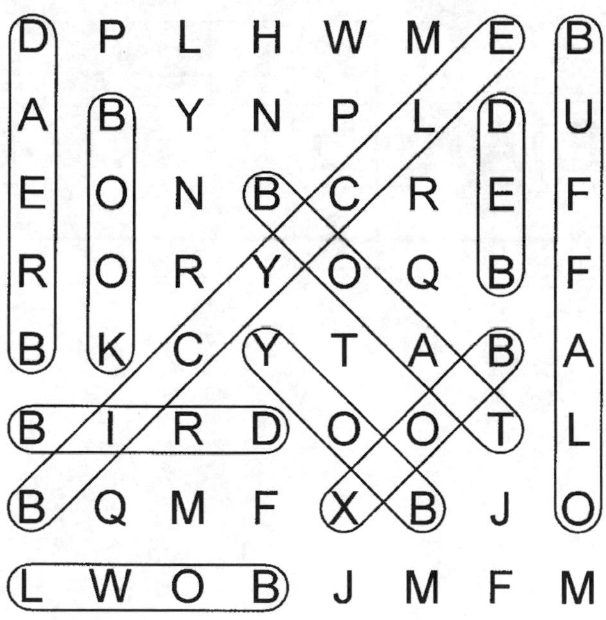

A Children's Picture-Word and Simple Sentence Book Crossword Puzzle

Solution:

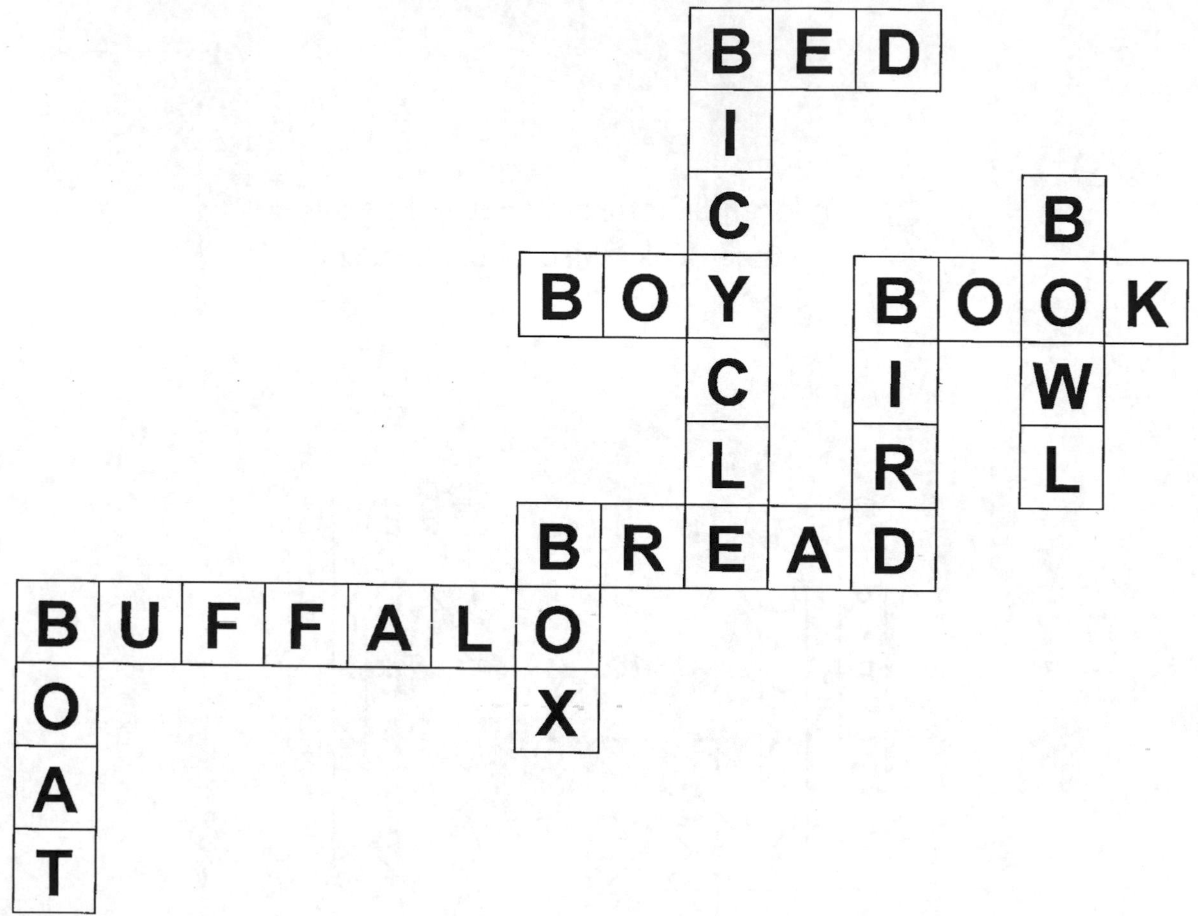

A Children's Picture-Word and Simple Sentence Book Word Search Puzzle

A Children's Picture-Word and Simple Sentence Book Crossword Puzzle

Solution:

A Children's Picture-Word and Simple Sentence Book Word Search Puzzle

A Children's Picture-Word and Simple Sentence Book Crossword Puzzle

Solution:

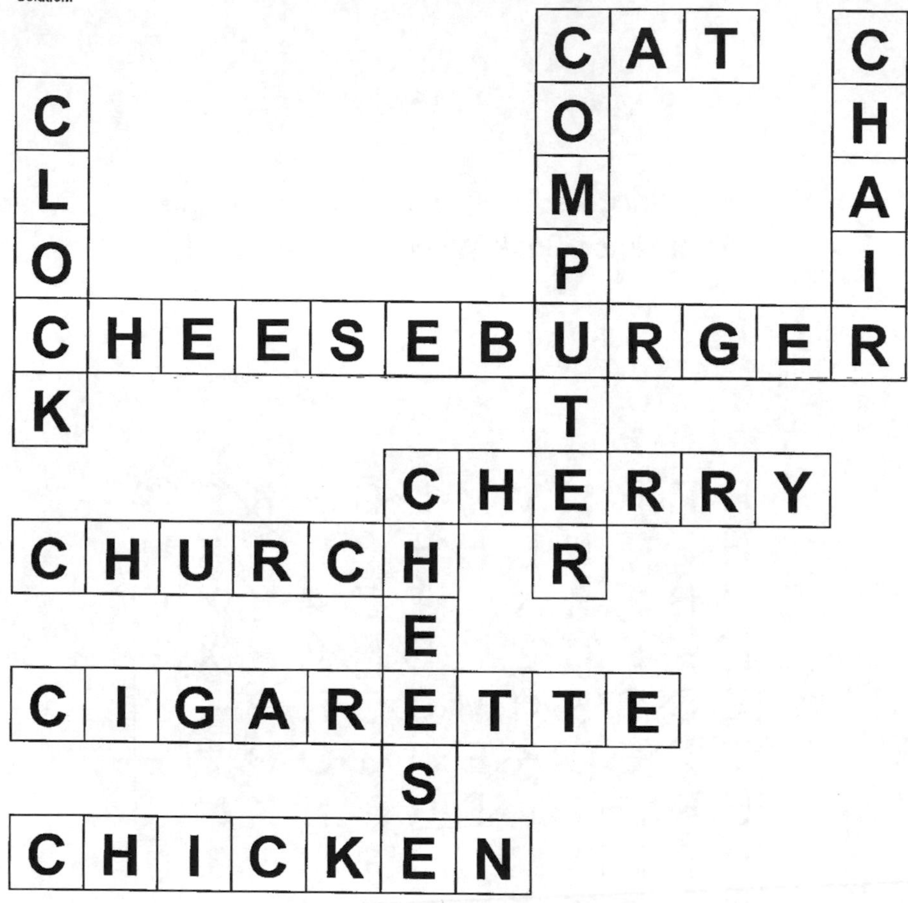

A Children's Picture-Word and Simple Sentence Book Word Search Puzzle

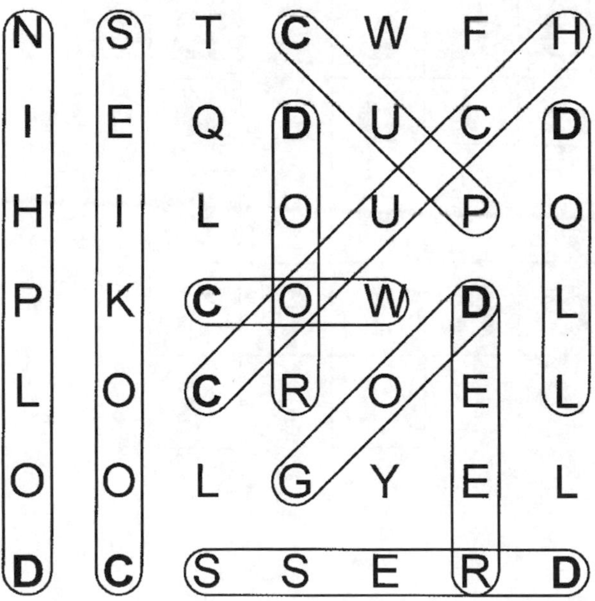

A Children's Picture-Word and Simple Sentence Book Crossword Puzzle

Solution:

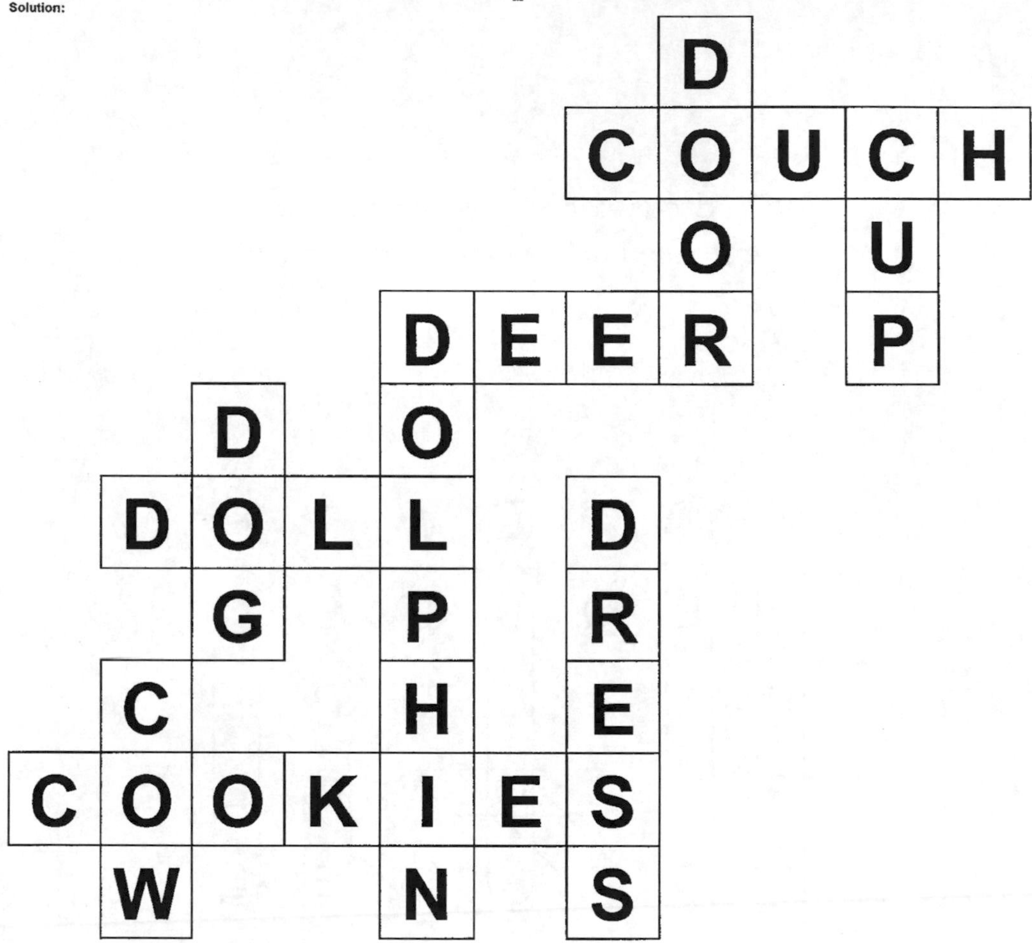

A Children's Picture-Word and Simple Sentence Book Word Search Puzzle

A Children's Picture-Word and Simple Sentence Book Crossword Puzzle

Solution:

A Children's Picture-Word and Simple Sentence Book Word Search Puzzle

A Children's Picture-Word and Simple Sentence Book Crossword Puzzle

Solution:

A Children's Picture-Word and Simple Sentence Book Word Search Puzzle

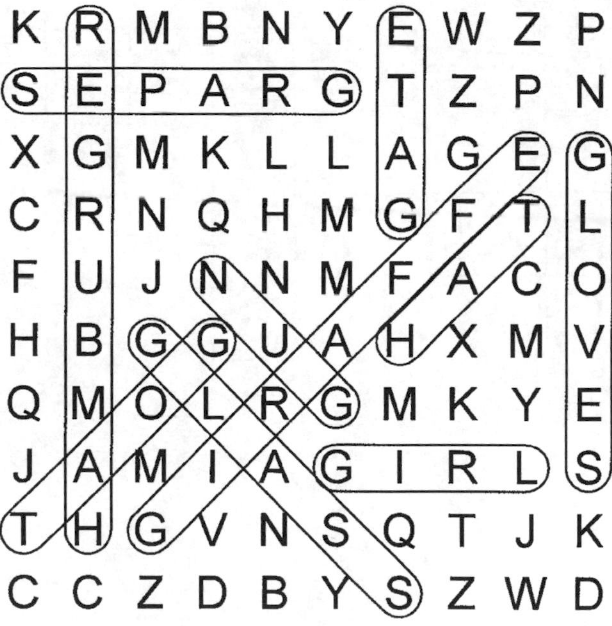

A Children's Picture-Word and Simple Sentence Book Crossword Puzzle

Solution:

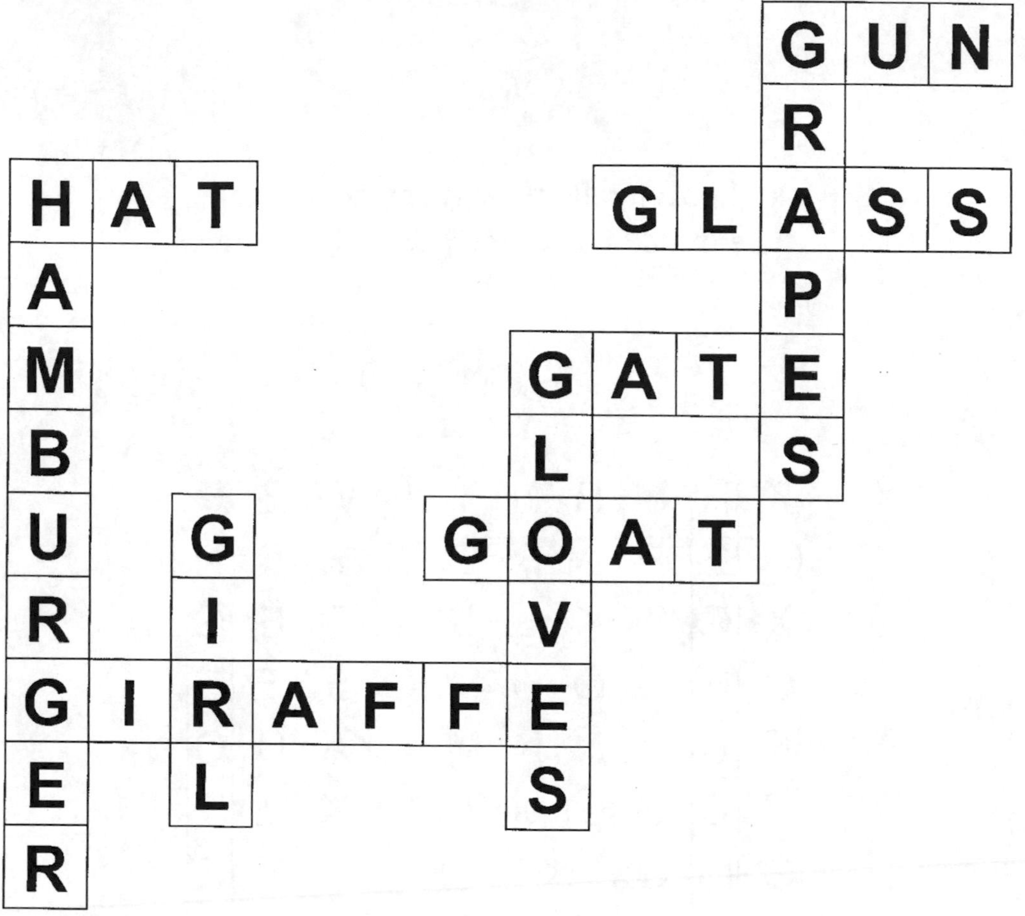

A Children's Picture-Word and Simple Sentence Book Word Search Puzzle

A Children's Picture-Word and Simple Sentence Book Crossword Puzzle

Solution:

		J	A	C	K	E	T				
		E									K
		L		J							A
		L		U							N
K	E	Y		I		H	O	T	D	O	G
I		F		C		O					A
T		I	C	E	C	R	E	A	M		R
E		S				S					O
		H	O	U	S	E					O

A Children's Picture-Word and Simple Sentence Book Word Search Puzzle

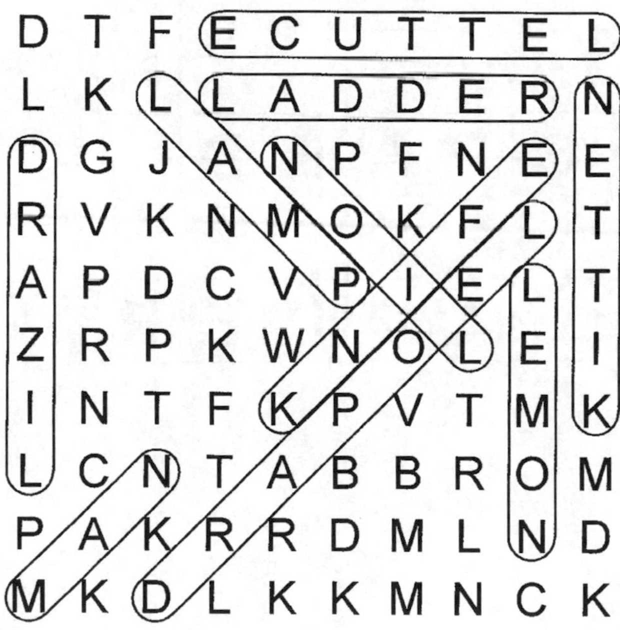

A Children's Picture-Word and Simple Sentence Book Crossword Puzzle

Solution:

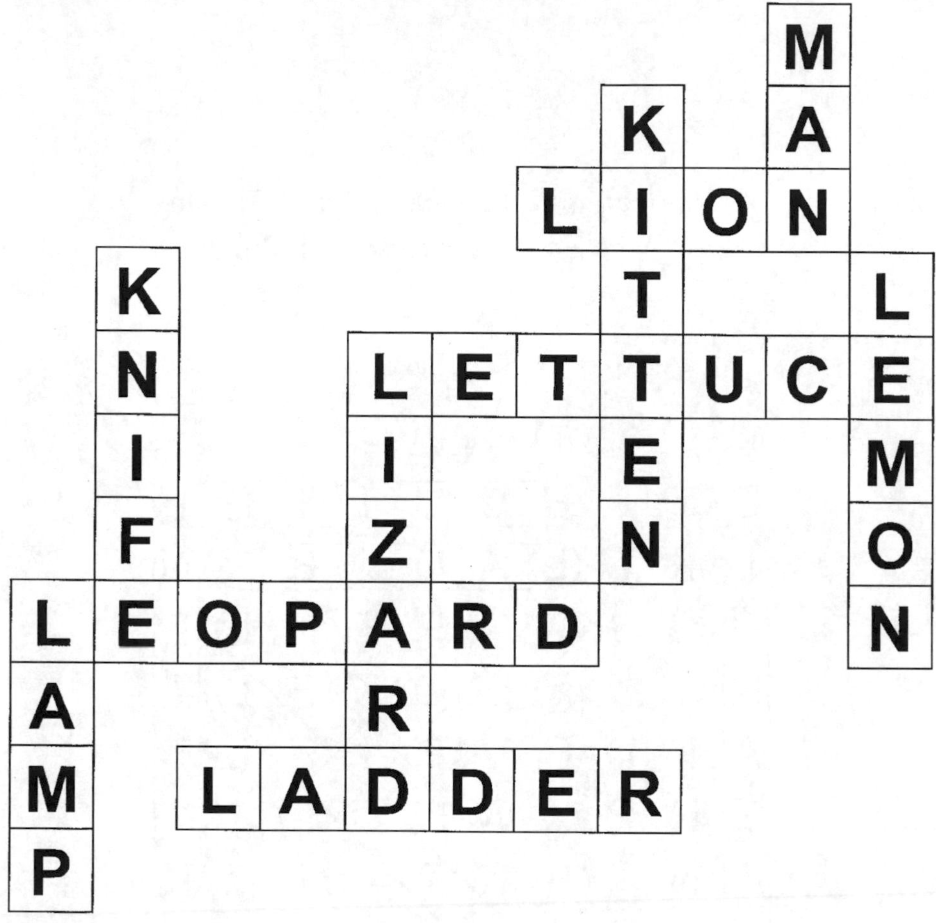

A Children's Picture-Word and Simple Sentence Book Word Search Puzzle

A Children's Picture-Word and Simple Sentence Book Crossword Puzzle

Solution:

A Children's Picture-Word and Simple Sentence Book Word Search Puzzle

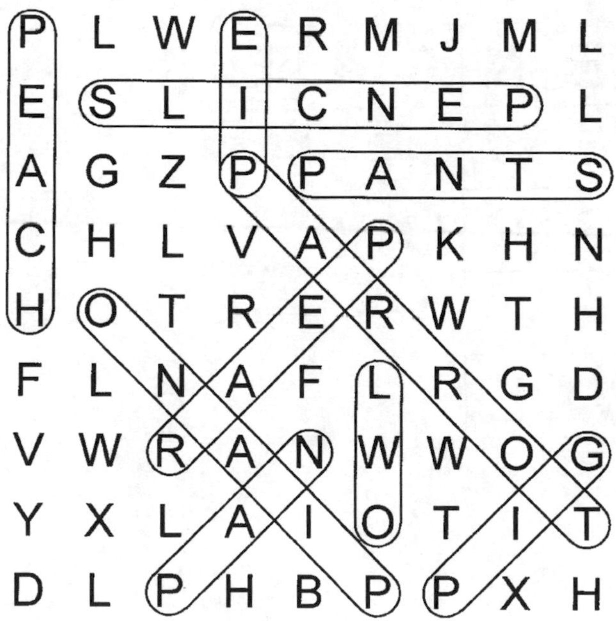

A Children's Picture-Word and Simple Sentence Book Crossword Puzzle

Solution:

A Children's Picture-Word and Simple
Sentence Book Word Search Puzzle

A Children's Picture-Word and Simple Sentence Book Crossword Puzzle

Solution:

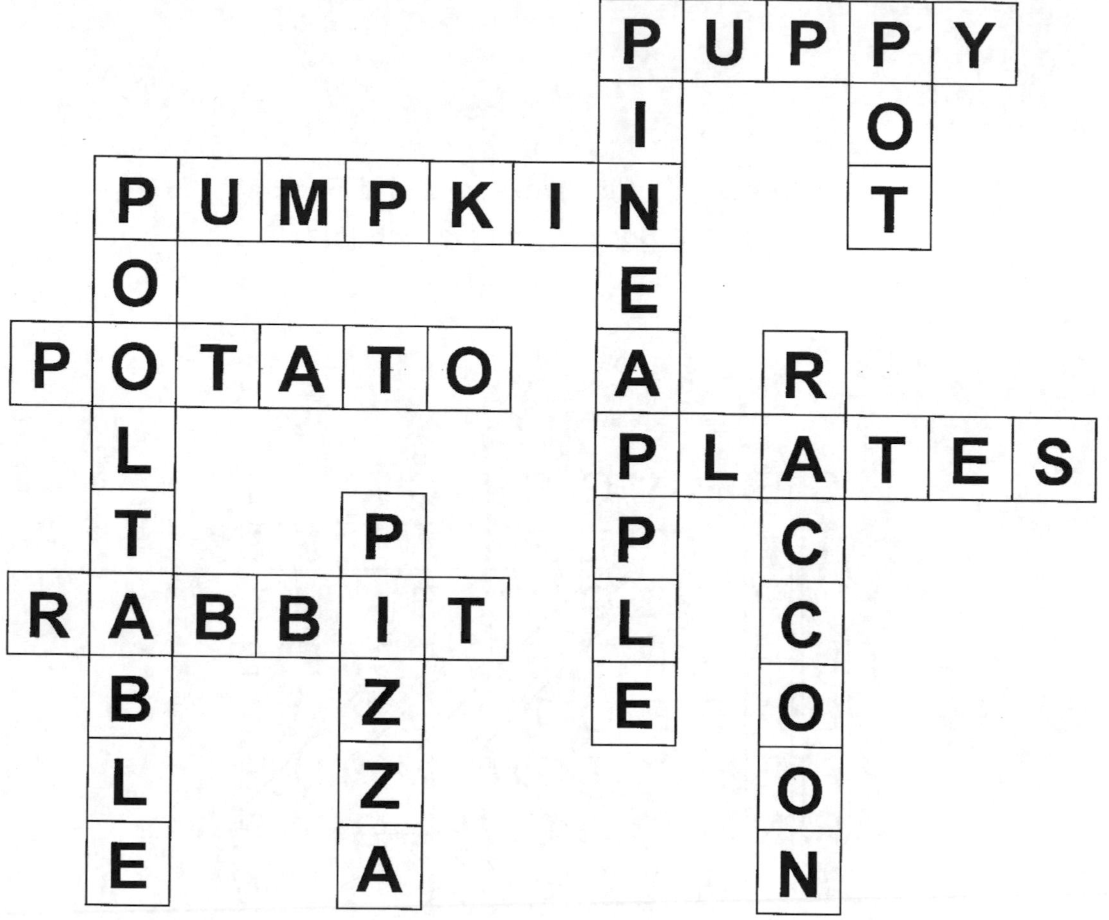

A Children's Picture-Word and Simple Sentence Book Word Search Puzzle

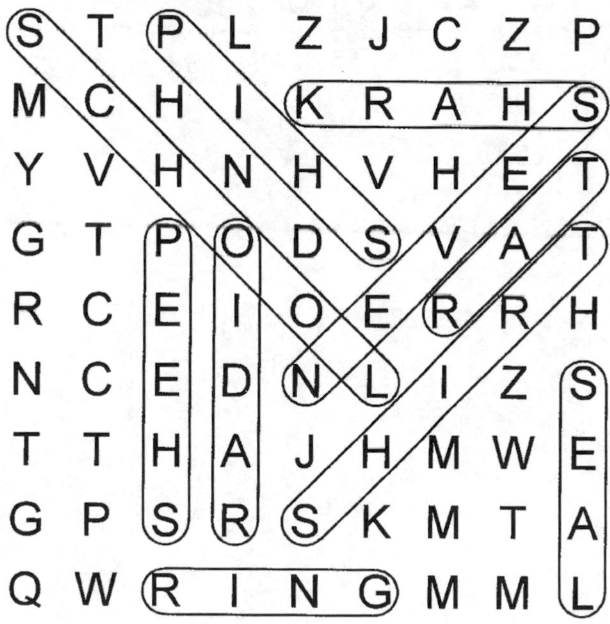

A Children's Picture-Word and Simple Sentence Book Crossword Puzzle

Solution:

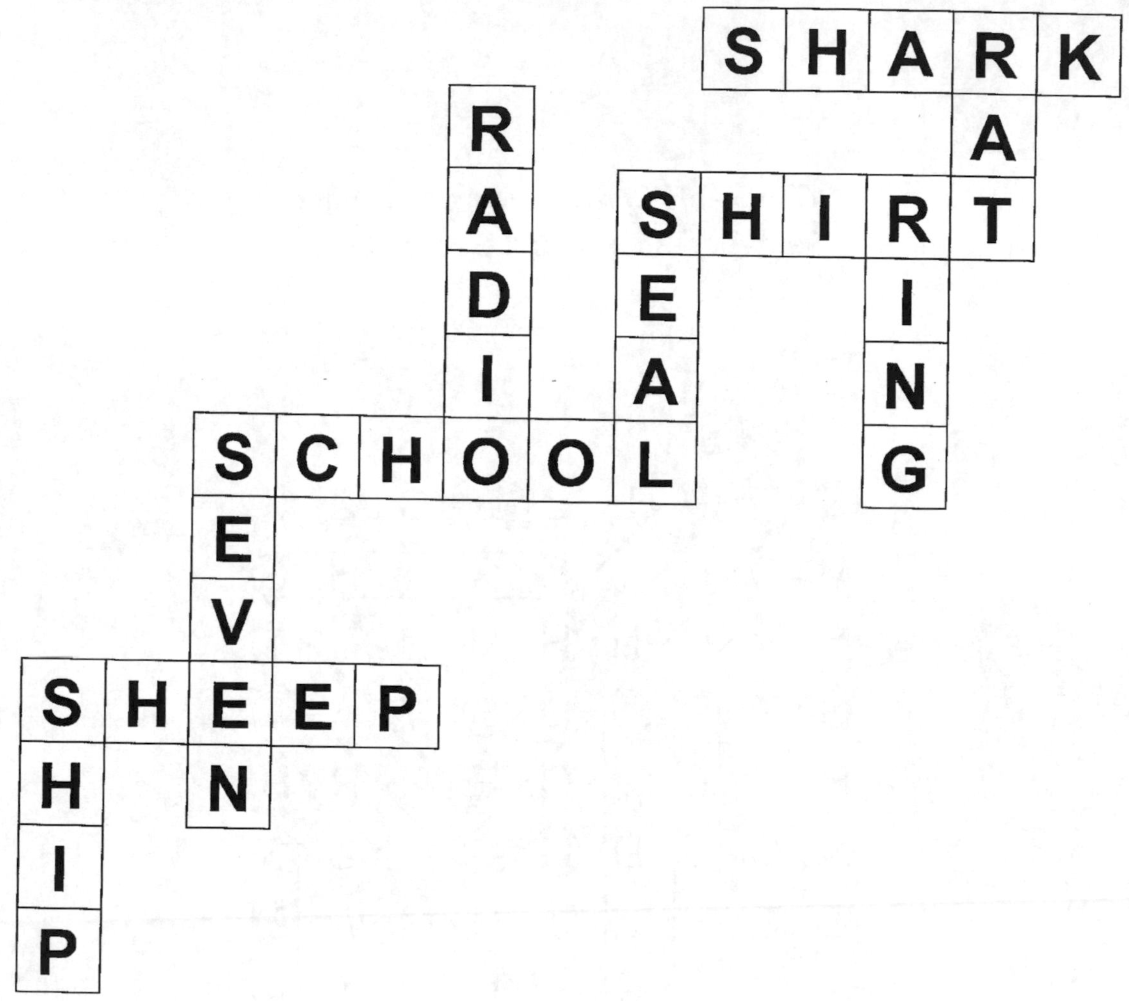

A Children's Picture-Word and Simple Sentence Book Word Search Puzzle

A Children's Picture-Word and Simple Sentence Book Crossword Puzzle

Solution:

SOCKS, SKELETON, SNAKE, SKUNK, SPOON, SNAIL, SKIRT, SIX, SHOES, SKY

A Children's Picture-Word and Simple Sentence Book Word Search Puzzle

A Children's Picture-Word and Simple Sentence Book Crossword Puzzle

Solution:

STOVE
TEDDYBEAR
TELEVISION
SUNGLASSES
TABLE
SQUIRREL
SWIMMINGPOOL
SUN
TEN
TELEPHONE

A Children's Picture-Word and Simple Sentence Book Word Search Puzzle

A Children's Picture-Word and Simple Sentence Book Crossword Puzzle

Solution:

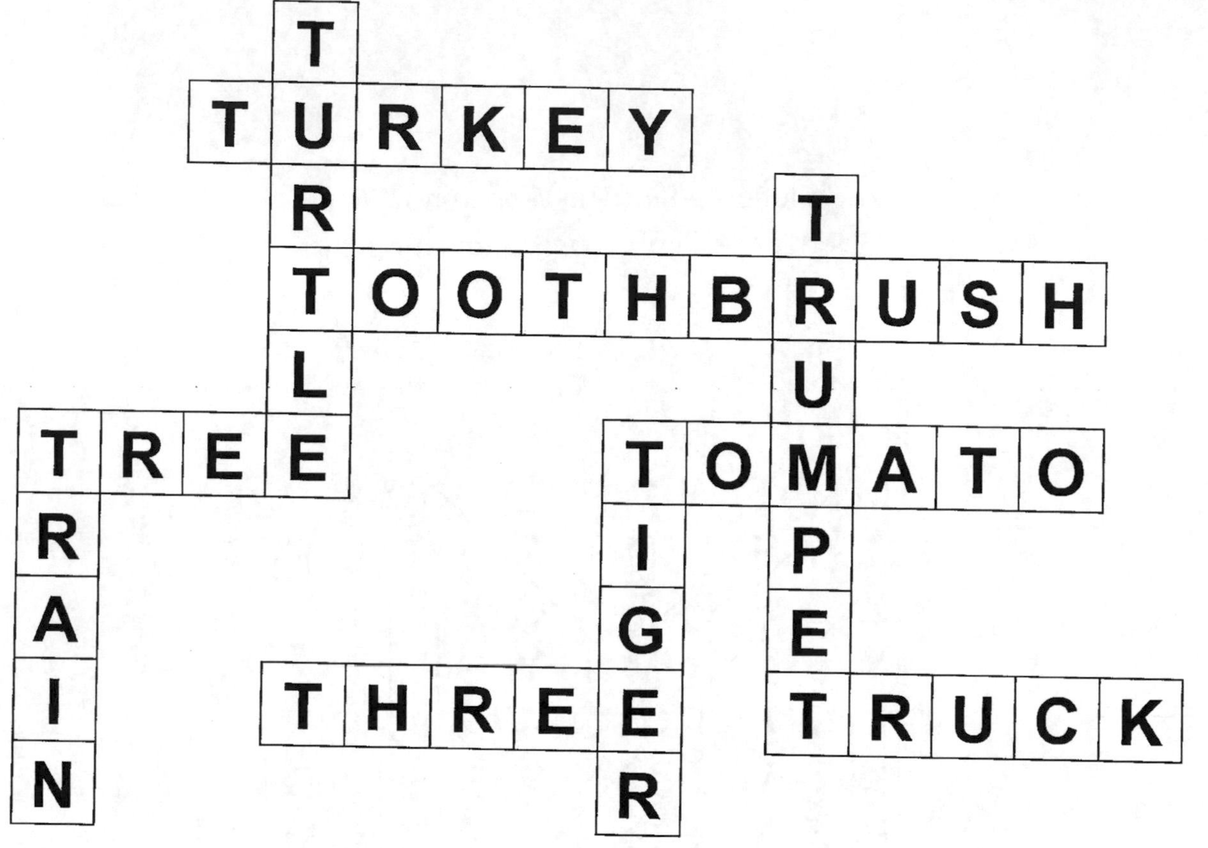

A Children's Picture-Word and Simple Sentence Book Word Search Puzzle

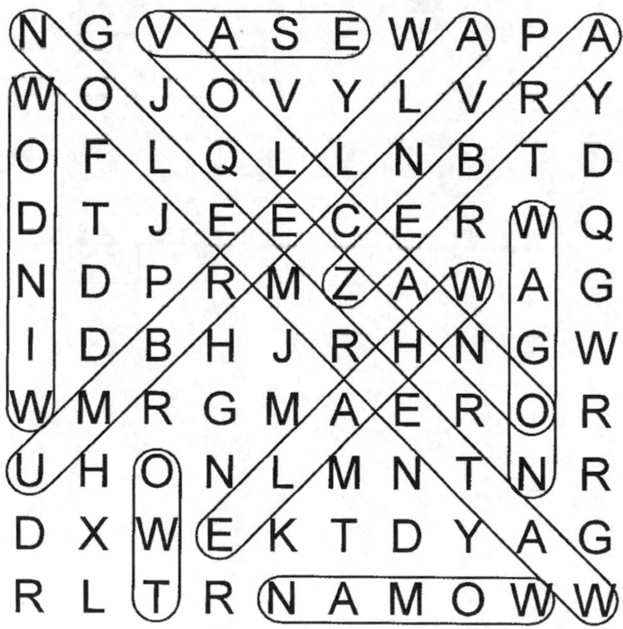

A Children's Picture-Word and Simple Sentence Book Crossword Puzzle

Solution:

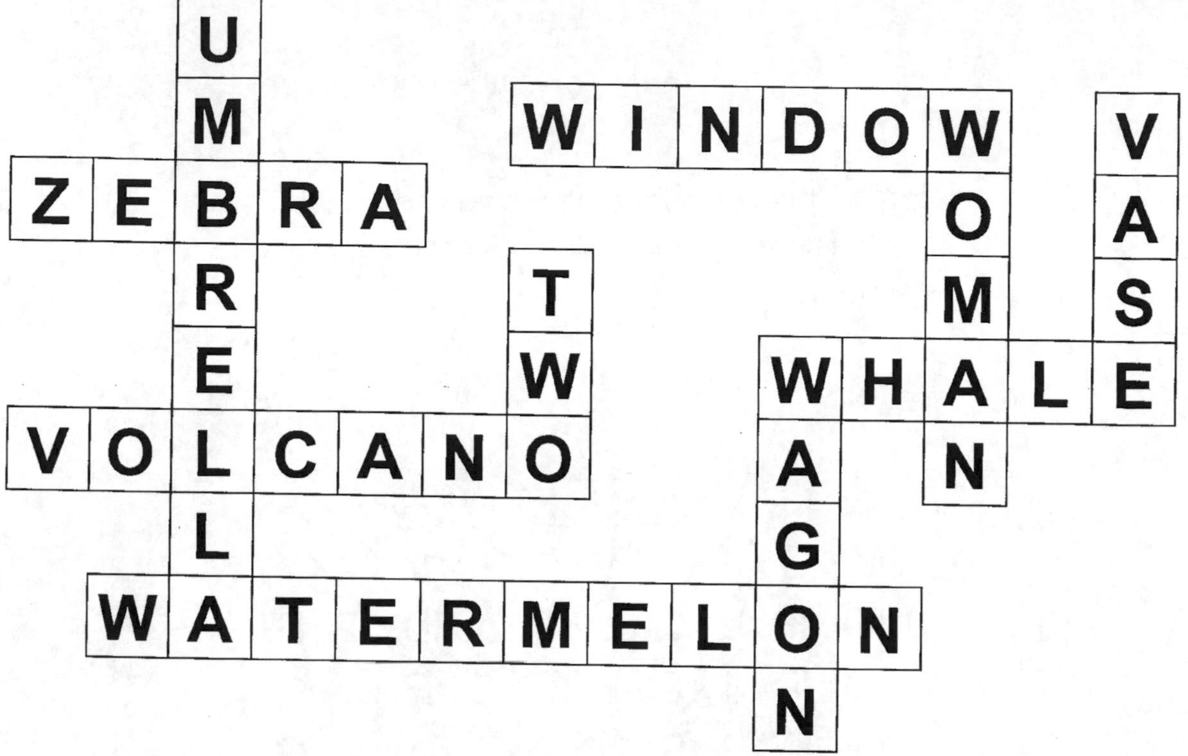

Order this book online at www.trafford.com
or email orders@trafford.com

Most Trafford titles are also available at major online book retailers.

Note for Librarians: A cataloguing record for this book is available from Library and Archives Canada at www.collectionscanada.ca/amicus/index-e.html

Printed in Victoria, BC, Canada.

ISBN: 978-1-4269-0658-9 (sc)

ISBN: 978-1-4269-0660-2 (e-book)

Our mission is to efficiently provide the world's finest, most comprehensive book publishing service, enabling every author to experience success. To find out how to publish your book, your way, and have it available worldwide, visit us online at www.trafford.com

Trafford rev. 1/12/2010

www.trafford.com

North America & international
toll-free: 1 888 232 4444 (USA & Canada)
phone: 250 383 6864 • fax: 812 355 4082